SOCIAL SKILLS GAMES FOR TEENS AND ADULTS WITH ASPERGER´S SYNDROME
50 games and dynamics to work on relationships, communication, trust, and other key social skills

Sandra J. Rogers

Copyright © Sandra J. Rogers 2021
All Rights Reserved

TABLE OF CONTENT

FOREWORD 6
GROUP DYNAMICS TO WORK ON SOCIAL SKILLS 11
1 THE MIRROR 13
2 PASSING THE BALL 15
3 PICTIONARY 17
4 SHARING BY TEACHING 19
5 FILM CLIPS 22
6 CREATION OF SCHEDULES 24
7 MIMES TELL ME HOW I FEEL 26
8 WE READ A STORY 28
9 TREASURE HUNT 30
10 DEBATES 32
11 DRAMATIZING THE INTERVIEW 34
12 PERFORMING TASKS 36
13 THE SPIDER'S WEB 38
14 DRAW YOUR PARTNER 41
15 THE BROKEN TELEPHONE 43
16 THE BOAT SINKS 45
17 I CREATE BY PAINTING AND BUILDING 47
20 POINTS TABLE 49
21 FOLLOW THE TRACK 51
22 FIVE AT A TIME 54
23 FIND YOUR PARTNER 56
24 THROUGH MIMICRY 58
25 WINDMILLS 60
26 THE MEETING 62
27 THERE IS TIME FOR EVERYTHING 64
28 WHAT DO I KNOW? 66
29 TRIPLE ANSWER 68

30 BALL WITH PHRASES 70

31 CHANGING THINGS AROUND 72

32 THE CLOCK 74

33 THE APARTMENT 76

34 FREE YOURSELF FROM ANGER 78

35 THE ANGER BOX 80

36 THE VOLCANO 83

37 I CALM DOWN 85

38 GAME OF COLORS 88

39 ASSEMBLE THE CASTLE 90

40 THE TURTLE 92

41 WHAT IS MISSING? 94

42 FOLLOW THE FOOTPRINT 97

43 COLORED RINGS 99

44 CREATE THE GARLAND 101

45 WHAT TIME IS IT, MR. WOLF? 103

46 THE HAT 106

47 PEPITO GOT SICK 108

48 THE MOTORCYCLE 110

49 CONDUCTING THE ORCHESTRA 112

50 FLYING 114

FOREWORD

Asperger's syndrome (AS) is a developmental disorder that is part of the autism spectrum according to the DSM-5 (Diagnostic and Statistical Manual of Mental Disorders of the American Psychiatric Association), therefore it is not considered a distinct syndrome, rather a mild or very mild autism.

It affects social interaction and verbal and non-verbal communication of the sufferer. In addition, there is a resistance to adapt to changes as well as an inflexibility of thought and difficulty to assume narrow and dominant fields of interests.

Professor Pedro Padrón Pulido, a scholar of the subject due to his influence within the classroom, stated in 2012 that people with Asperger syndrome manifest behavior with repetitive traits, limited interests and motor clumsiness.

Nevertheless, people with AS are very intelligent and have great memory and tend to excel in science and mathematics. A person with mild symptoms can live in their environment without any inconvenience and go unnoticed, so to be considered with the syndrome, severe symptoms must be present.

Attwood and Lienas Massot, teacher and writer, stated in 2009 through a guide on this syndrome, that the diagnosis usually appears at the beginning of school, approximately, from the age of three. They indicate that for people with ASdaily exchange with the surrounding environment does not represent a major difficulty, but problem arises when they come into contact with their peers and socialization takes place

AS is more common than other types of autism, being considered a rare condition of which very few people, even professionals know about, and therefore do not have the necessary experience to treat it.

There are no exact causes to it, but these are attributed, more generally, to genetic/hereditary reasons. However, it is also worth considering risk factors that exist, which are presented below:

- Family history, generally, in half of the cases a genetic component plays a part.

- Fragile X syndrome and Rett syndrome.

- Premature babies, those born before 26 weeks of gestation.

- Suffering from tuberous sclerosis.

Additionally, it should be noted that most children suffering from Asperger are boys, because it is easier to diagnose for them, their ability to adapt, according to Josep Artigas, a Spanish specialist in neuropediatric and psychology.

When referring to AS, it should be considered that it is differentiated between infantile, adolescent and adult, being these the different stages in which it is identified.

Symptoms of Asperger's syndrome

Symptoms may be present depending on the age of the person, since these are changeable.

At the infantile stage, children show greater ability for memory and language different than other children of the same age.

They adapt very easily to routines because they are disciplined, but may present bad behavior due to frustrations and anxiety produced by certain situations.

In adolescence, their disinterest in establishing personal relationships with other children increases, although they adapt better and much faster to social rules.

They themselves set the routines to be fulfilled, mainly because it is a habit that they have assumed since childhood. They have absorbing interests and their vocabulary and language is clear and impeccable.

They do not do very well with motor activities and are clumsy; they are emotionally immature and not good at expressing their feelings.

It may seem that the emotions of other people do not have great importance, however, it is not so, it is just that they have a hard time identifying these in others and therefore understand what is happening.

On the other hand, it is difficult for them to adapt to the educational system due to the changes of study centers, teachers and schedules.

They are very noble people without malice. Do not support unfair criticism and become defenders of human rights.

Symptoms in adulthood are noted by the difficulty to have friends, to establish intimate relationships as well as to adapt to work due to their lack of attention. They present limitations to understand non-verbal language, they are also very undisciplined at planning future projects.

They suffer from anxiety and depression; they are impulsive precisely because they do not find a way to express what is happening to them or what they are feeling.

With regard to their goals, if these are clear, they are persistent until achieving them.

It is worth noting that in all three stages they have very little tolerance to environmental conditions such as noises, smells, tastes and lights, they are sensitive and so do not expose themselves to them.

Living with an Asperger person

Living with and dealing with a child or adolescent who suffers from this condition is not easy, especially because it is necessary to understand them and to know strategies that would allow adapting to their situation and responding to their demands.

For Juan Martos, a psychologist graduated from the Universidad Autónoma de Madrid, in order to understand the behavior of others "we must be able to put ourselves in their place" only then is it possible to understand the reactions or thoughts that lead them to act in a certain way.

For this reason, among the many ways that can be considered to learn to live with an Asperger person, is to be empathetic, to put ourselves in their place and in the situations that are difficult for them to cope with in order to achieve an understanding of what happens to them.

Knowing the person well, their likes and dislikes, conversations of interest, weaknesses and strengths will contribute to improve relationships;

understanding what is important to them, you will discover tools that allow you to socialize and make them feel comfortable.

When talking, it is necessary to express yourself clearly and directly. Sometimes it is necessary to explain some specific definitions in relation to what you want to transmit, so that they can gain a better understanding.

It is important to understand that their way of behaving and expressing themselves are not caprices, but a way to make themselves understood by others.

It is important to understand what is valuable to them and only if it is necessary try to make changes. This modification should be made using pertinent strategies, without imposing points of view that are contrary to what they consider to be their rightful positions.

There are a number of difficulties that tend to arise in relation to their environment, each according to their stage. For the main ones addressed in this section, the infantile and adolescent stages, is incorporating tools useful in any context.

In order to achieve this objective, a series of dynamics are proposed below, each of them adapted to the realities that may face children and young people with ASin everyday life.

GROUP DYNAMICS TO WORK ON SOCIAL SKILLS

Social skills are recognized as the set of behaviors that an individual possesses to relate with others efficiently.

Based on this definition, Manuel Vieites, philosopher and doctor in educational sciences, stated in 2009, that every child must acquire competences that make him/her capable of understanding and interacting in the world with his/her peers in an assertive way, respecting cultural and thought differences, as well as exercising his/her rights and responsibilities.

As is well known, children and adolescents with AS present some difficulty in establishing interpersonal relationships.

Their relationship skills are scarce, thus their emotional and social responses may not be the most appropriate. Because of this, it is very likely that they do not feel the desire to share their knowledge and experiences with others.

Eduardo Arango Tobón, who is a researcher and teacher, stated in 1998 that dynamic activity is the main tasks of children and adolescents, by participating they learn to deal with the world around them and acquire skills to interact with the environment.

While children or adolescents with AS may not engage in imitative social games and imaginative activities like other children, they are not exempt from participating and enriching themselves with the socializing strategies that these activities offer.

But to help further assist them, the following dynamics can be used:

1
THE MIRROR

Materials needed for this dynamic: mirror

Minimum number of people: between 15 and 20 people.

Time: approximately 15 minutes

Children with AS are very good at using examples, so this dynamic of imitation can contribute to their integration by learning different skills and sequences of behaviors that they can then put into practice.

Establishing pairs or groups, one of the people must stand in front of the Asperger child and perform an action, the rest of the group must carefully observe every detail of the action and imitate it.

It is worth noting that the actions should start with a very simple gesture and then increase the level of complexity, i.e., from very easy to very difficult. The idea is for the child to follow the sequence of each one while imitating them and perfecting his mastery and technique.

With the dynamic, it is possible to perceive that imitating, making mistakes, laughing are all part of it, trying until person has participated. This will allow the child to initiate a time of interaction with the group opening up to sharing and acquiring social skills.

These actions provide the child or adolescent with tools that gradually allow him/her to integrate into the group. By discovering these ways of relating, it will be much easier to apply them in other contexts while providing the opportunity to establish interpersonal relationships.

In addition, it favors communication and emotional connection. Once a child with AS opens a thread of trust with someone it will be much easier for him/her to socialize in a new opportunity.

2
PASSING THE BALL

Materials needed for this dynamic: ball

Minimum number of people: between 15 and 20 people.

Time: 20 minutes approximately

The dynamic is very simple. You must have a ball in hand and all members of the group, whether family or class should be placed in a circle next to each other. A captain is selected who will be responsible for giving instructions and start the game.

Instructions must be precise and very detailed. If the Asperger members do not understand something, given their lack of understanding of the rules of social interaction, it must be patiently explained again how the dynamics will be developed.

The ball should be passed little by little to each of the participants, that is to say, everyone should come into contact with the ball, it should not necessarily be passed to the person next to you, you can choose who you want to give it to and throw it from one place to another.

The important thing is that, with the ball in hand and before passing it, a very particular characteristic of the person who is going to receive it is expressed. This cycle will be repeated over and over again until everyone has participated and listened to the characteristics that were expressed among themselves.

The captain will be in charge of verifying that all members intervene and will indicate when to stop the game.

At the end there will be a space for interaction so that everyone can give their point of view in relation to the characteristics of each partner and if they wish they can add something else. The AS child/children will be able to enter into a relationship and communication process as part of the skills they can adopt to socialize.

3
PICTIONARY

Materials needed for this dynamic: pencil, paper, markers.

Minimum number of people: between 15 and 20 people.

Time: approximately 20 minutes

For Asperger's children it is difficult to work with imitation. With this dynamic the aim is to stimulate the capacity for interpretation in communication with the other, favoring expression through language as well as interpersonal skills.

The game consists of forming pairs. There should always be a captain who is in charge of explaining instructions, so that everyone can understand and achieve the objectives

A pencil and paper should be provided. If they are in the classroom, a blackboard and chalk can be used. By drawing one member of the pair tries to transmit a message that the other member must decipher and interpret it.

Messages to be conveyed can be related to something you like, something you do not like or simply a phrase that the person who draws wants to convey to his partner.

If a blackboard is used where everyone can see the drawing, no one should give a clue, even if they discover the message, before the pair person does it.

Once the dynamic is completed, a discussion should be held to present the benefits of the exercise and what has been learned through it.

Some questions that can be asked after the exercise are: How did you feel not being able to express yourself in words? Did you find it more complicated to do it by drawing or easier?

The Aspergers present will feel motivated to express themselves, and that is the goal pursued: to open a path of interaction with the other where they can discover the richness of relating, thus reducing the feelings of frustration when notable to.

It is important to emphasize that in developing these activities the leader must be very patient. Not all children have the ability to understand easily or quickly.

Each child is different, therefore requires different stimulation, and in the case of AS children, this situation is even more acute.

4
SHARING BY TEACHING

Materials needed for this dynamic: notebook or book.

Minimum number of people: from 4 people

Time: 20 minutes approximately

For children and adolescents with Asperger's it is very practical to talk about their topics of interest.

In this dynamic, the child with the condition takes the place of the teacher. He/she will be able to express his/her knowledge and interest about something researched and mastered well. A captain should be selected to lead the dynamic in order to guarantee the order and the time allotted for it.

This latter point is extremely important; it should be remembered that children who present this condition, in general, when allowed to talk about a topic they are passionate about, they know when to start, but not when to finish.

The group should stand in a circle around him/her. With notebooks in hand, he/she takes on the role and begins to explain.

His classmates should listen attentively and at the end ask for the right to intervene sharing opinions related to the topic. The idea is to generate an exchange of opinions where the Asperger child or adolescent can show his skills and leadership ability.

As he/she notices the interest of the participants in relation to what he/she has exposed, he/she will be motivated and will continue expressing his/her ideas, until the captain or leader indicates that the dynamic has concluded.

To stimulate learning, at the end a space is opened to talk about the importance of establishing interpersonal relationships and learning the points of view of other people. The key learning is socializing and feeding on the knowledge that others express.

Group dynamics to work on managing emotions

Children and adolescents with Asperger's syndrome are not very prone to show emotions. They have a hard time being empathic, so they choose to be simple and direct regardless of the fact that they may generate discomfort in others.

Dziobek Isabel, psychologist, stated in 2006, that people with Asperger's syndrome present a difficulty in the amygdala which is part of the syndrome's own manifestations. Among them, difficulties in emotional regulation and social interaction stand out.

As a consequence, when they find themselves in a situation in which they do not know how to express themselves, they explode in anger. Through these dynamics, the aim is to offer tools that allow them to identify what they feel before certain events and what is the best way to express it.

Once they manage to learn to channel their emotions, they will be able to establish bonds of greater interaction with others, so when they find themselves in situations that trigger emotions, they will feel more confident to explain what affects them.

5
FILM CLIPS

Materials needed for this dynamic: film to visualize and resource to do so. Posters with images

Minimum number of people: 20 and 25 people.

Time: approximately 30 to 45 minutes

The use of short movie fragments help children and adolescents with Asperger's to identify and improve the ways in which emotions are handled.

Beforehand, it is explained what emotions are, how they are identified and some characteristics related to them. The group is told that for the next meeting they should watch the selected movie (at which point the name should be provided).

While watching it, they have the task of taking notes of elements that are directly related to emotions.

Once gathered, the group is placed in a circle, sitting next to each other, and they are given cards or posters with images of faces that represent an emotion: joy, sadness, anxiety, nervousness, fear, anger, etc. The cards are passed around one by one.

Then a space is opened to talk about the film and the characteristics they wrote down and their relationship with the posters and images.

The Asperger child or adolescent is asked to assign a poster to the scenes he/she observed and to relate them to the different emotions.

When he/she achieves the objective, he/she will be able to learn to identify his/her own emotions, and will be able to understand when he/she is sad or happy, afraid, anxious, angry, stressed, etc.

Finally, a conclusion should be made that emotions are born with every human being, that they are not bad or harmful as long as we learn how to channel them.

Tools and exercises that allow them to achieve this task are provided and a space is opened for them to express how they felt and the learnings acquired during the development of the dynamics.

6
CREATION OF SCHEDULES

Materials needed for this dynamic: paper, sheets of paper and colors.

Minimum number of people: 20 and 25 people.

Time: approximately 30 minutes

For children and adolescents with AS, the establishment of rules and routines are of great importance, thus they keep a record of what is going to happen, thus reducing stress and anxiety levels.

Organizing people in groups. Each one is instructed to take note of the activities they perform on a daily basis organizing them in order of priority.

Once this first part has been explained and carried out, the importance of organizing duties that are performed daily is discussed in order to consider the fulfillment of each and every one of them without overlooking any of them.

Orientations are given to elaborate schedules, they can make them in tables, writing by order of importance and time each event. They can be accompanied with drawings or images that decorate them and make them be more attractive.

At the end of the activity, there is time to explain the activity developed, as well as to share how they felt, giving order and form to the activities carried out.

This game provides security to children and adolescents with AS, as it reduces the fear of events that have not yet happened and helps them to manage the emotions generated by the timely fulfillment of each commitment.

7
MIMES TELL ME HOW I FEEL

Materials needed for this exercise: paper, markers, blackboard.

Minimum number of people: 20 and 25 people.

Time: 30 to 45 minutes approximately

Children and adolescents with Asperger's present great difficulty in recognizing the feelings in others, many times they do not seem to care, but the truth is that they do not have the tools to identify them and much less to react to them in a timely manner.

For this reason, it is essential to work on this recognition to better interact in their environment.

The game consists of placing all the members of the group in circles in order to develop the representation of specific emotional states using modeling.

The Asperger's child or adolescent is a target participant. The group leader chooses an emotion to represent through mime, then through an example, explains the group the situation. The ASchild, who is the chosen participant, try to guess.

He/she can ask his/her peers for clues and, among different opinions, try to guess the emotions represented.

Once he/she manages to find the emotion, he/she will be asked to try to make the representation for the rest of the group to guess.

At the end, a small reflection is made about the importance of knowing what the other feels and being able to understand it, so that interpersonal relationships are meaningful for all parties.

8
WE READ A STORY

Materials needed for this dynamic: story, posters with images.

Minimum number of people: 20 and 25 people.

Time: 30 to 45 minutes approximately

For this dynamic, a reading comprehension activity will be developed to allow the AS child or adolescent to identify what he/she reads with emotions.

Participants are asked to stand in a circle, sitting side by side. The leader begins the reading, while everyone must listen carefully, the particular aspect is that story is related to the emotions of each of its characters.

The intention is that the Asperger child or adolescent can understand that the other also experiences emotions.

Once the reading is finished, a series of questions will be asked to the participants, which will be directly related to the emotions expressed by the characters.

When it is the child's turn, he/she will have to put him/herself in the place of each of the characters in order to identify what each of them was feeling.

Then, a traffic light with its different colors and posters with emotions identified with the colors of the traffic light will be provided. Participants will have to select each one of them and place it in the traffic light in the corresponding color.

At the end, it will be ensured that all group participants have managed to understand and identify the emotions that human beings have and will be oriented to the appropriate management of them.

Group dynamics to work on the difficulty of making friends

The issue of making friends seems to be unimportant for children and adolescents with Asperger Syndrome.

But the reality is that they are people who do not have enough tools to interact with others and much less to open spaces of trust to establish more personal relationships and achieve a bond of friendship.

This can result in a state of frustration and trigger aggression and anxiety. Appropriate guidance should be given to overcome this internal conflict and help improve relationships.

According to the DSM - 5, among the characteristics that people with Asperger syndrome present is the absence of the spontaneous tendency to share enjoyment, interests and objectives with other people.

Performing a well-organized work can contribute to create spaces where they can feel that they are in considered and what is important for him/her is also important for the other.

9
TREASURE HUNT

Materials needed for this activity: different objects found where the activity is to be carried out.

Minimum number of people: 20 and 25 people.

Time: approximately 40 minutes

A leader or captain is chosen who will be in charge of giving guidance. He/she should organize the group in pairs, the idea is that they work together and in complicity to achieve the objective. The group will be asked to leave the space dedicated to the game for five minutes and then return.

The leader/captain will take the objects that are available in the space that are small and light and hide them in strategic places, and then indicates to the group that they can enter again.

Working in pairs as a unit, they have to find all the objects that were hidden. This will allow the Asperger child or adolescent to understand that it is possible to trust each other and that when there are common interests, personal relationships can be established that will allow them to achieve the proposed objective.

They will be able to see their partner as an ally with whom they can work with empathy when having the necessary tools.

The closing should be done with a small conclusion about the importance and benefits of being able to trust other people and establish bonds of friendship.

10
DEBATES

Materials needed for this dynamic: support material related to the topic to be discussed.

Minimum number of people: 20 and 25 people.

Time: 45 minutes approximately

For the development of this dynamic, the group is divided in two, and a captain is selected for each group to ensure its effective development.

We proceed to choose a relevant topic, which is current and of interest to everyone, including the Asperger's child or adolescent, as they are motivated to talk about those things that interest them.

It is explained to the two groups that winning will consist of teamwork, and that if any teammate has any doubts about what to answer, the others are there to help and support them.

Then they should proceed to write a series of questions in relation to the selected topic that they will ask the other group, these have to be of interest to both groups, as well as to each other, and also offer clear answers to each of them.

Once everything is organized, the debate will begin. Everyone must ask questions and everyone must answer, the team with the most correct answers will be the winner.

The objective is that Asperger children or adolescents open up to share in full confidence with the rest of the participants in the group, so they will feel the need to interact, ask, suggest, listen and sometimes respond to what the group suggests.

This will inspire confidence and will lead them to have an active and positive intervention hand in hand with the other, thus understanding that relationships of trust, harmony, empathy and respect that are established with others are necessary in our daily lives.

11
DRAMATIZING THE INTERVIEW

Materials needed for this dynamic: resources available in the space like tables, chairs, notepads, pens.

Minimum number of people: 20 and 25 people.

Time: approximately 45 minutes

For this exercise, the group of participants should be divided into pairs and the purpose of the exercise should be explained.

The idea is to choose a current and relevant topic to dramatize an interview, each pair should get together and write down the questions they want to ask the other person.

They can name the dynamics of an informative television program seen through the media or social networks.

The Asperger's child or adolescent can choose the role he/she wishes to play, either the interviewer or the interviewee; the interview will begin by giving him/her the opportunity to express him/herself about all the important elements he/she observes about the topic through questions and answers.

Generally, children and adolescents who suffer from this condition passionately talk about topics that are of interest to them, so adapting to this situation will not be complex for them.

With the development of the dynamic, he will be able to observe that what is important to him is also important to the other person. In this way, he/she will be able to establish bonds of greater trust for the next meetings.

At the end of the activity, it should be emphasized, especially so that the learning is well marked, that as human beings we always need each other and that in order to establish effective relationships, and therefore, it is necessary to create trusting spaces where we can work together and achieve our objectives.

For everyone it is essential to establish effective relationships, it is an innate need in every person, not only about teamwork, but beyond that, to be able to have someone to turn to at certain times.

Even though for children and adolescents with Asperger's this task is difficult, it is not impossible if they are provided with all the necessary tools and use all relevant strategies, it is possible that following certain guidelines they can strengthen friendships with other peers who may or may not suffer from the same condition.

12
PERFORMING TASKS

Materials needed for this dynamic: rulers, wastebaskets, first aid kit, others.

Minimum number of people: 20 and 25 people.

Time: 45 minutes approximately

Children and adolescents with Asperger's are very good at performing certain tasks. The purpose of this dynamic is to open a space of trust in order to establish agreements and work in a coordinated manner when faced with the need to carry out responsibilities with others.

The leader or captain will invite the group to form pairs and will indicate to each pair the responsibilities they will have to fulfill during the dynamics, establishing different committees for them, for example: discipline, cleanliness, health, safety, entertainment.

Establish a performance time for each pair; they will be in charge of keeping the routine in that space during the dynamic.

Members should meet before the beginning of the workshop to establish work criteria.

During this time, different episodes will have to be performed so that everyone can participate. A space will be destined to disorder. The couple in charge of discipline will have to work with the criteria they had established so that the group becomes orderly again.

Then, another space will be opened, someone from the group will have to express some kind of health discomfort, the couple in charge of the health committee will take place and will provide first aid.

In this way, everyone will have the opportunity to show their leadership as part of the committee assigned to them. All under the supervision of the leader.

At the end of the dynamic, emphasis will be placed on the importance of being able to work together to achieve a common good and that, to do so, not only coordination and organization are required, but also empathy and trust, fundamental values to strengthen bonds of friendship.

13
THE SPIDER'S WEB

Materials needed for this dynamic: yarn.

Minimum number of people: 20 and 25 people.

Time: 45 minutes approximately

This dynamic is widely used to open scenarios where it is possible to establish relationships with other people, knowing their characteristics and interests.

Children and adolescents with Asperger's may be interested in knowing what a peer is like, however, they will never take the initiative to ask. This dynamic is ideal for them to get to know each other and thus have the possibility of entering into scenarios of greater trust and empathy.

The group leader or captain will give the participants the orientation to sit in a circle, one next to the other.

Before starting the dynamic, he/she should carefully explain the way in which it will be developed in order to avoid disorder.

The captain starts the exercise with a roll of "pabilo" or yarn in hand, introduces himself by saying his name, a characteristic of his and something that is of interest to him. Example: "my name is Pedro, I am very funny and I like to dance."

Take the end of the yarn and throw the whole roll to the partner you want, the one who takes the roll, follows the dynamic: my name is, I am and I like, takes the end that corresponds to him and throws the roll to another member of the group.

This way the dynamic will continue until everyone has participated and a big spider has been formed, which will represent the union among them, together with the knowledge of their characteristics and interests that they surely did not know.

It is an ideal space to reflect on the need we have for each other, and that if given space to get to know each other, great friendships can be established.

Group dynamics to work on difficulties with imaginative and creative thinking

Children and adolescents with Asperger syndrome very often impose certain routines which can be quite rigid both for them and for their environment, they usually start from what they want to do, to what they want to eat during the day.

This reality can generate frustration in all those who accompany them in their process. Their inflexibility gives rise to difficulty with imaginative and creative thinking.

These routines however are changeable as they mature spaces of higher level of reasoning may open up.

Paul Harris, jurist and lawyer, writer of "Creativity, art, therapy and autism," stated in 2003, that subjects suffering from autism, show difficulties to perform a creative activity and do not develop the imaginative capacity or the ability to interpret the outside world.

For this reason, the different dynamics are intended to offer Asperger children and adolescents a number of tools that allow them to develop their imaginative and creative thinking, so that they can get out of the monotony generated by the daily practice of the same routine.

14
DRAW YOUR PARTNER

Materials needed for this dynamic: sheets of paper, pencils, markers.

Minimum number of people: 20 and 25 people.

Time: 45 minutes approximately

The development of this activity is intended for the AS child or adolescent to develop ideas and to be able to give rise to his or her imagination through drawing.

The group leader will divide the group into pairs, provide them with sheets of paper, pencils and markers, give instructions of the dynamic indicating to each participant that he/she must draw his/her partner. For this task he/she must take into account his/her characteristics as well as his/her interests.

Example: the AS child or adolescent will visualize if his partner is tall or short, fat or skinny, detail his features and take into account his interests, that is to say, he can draw him as he is and also if his partner likes to read, sing, dance, play, he will try to draw him in one of his activities or with some of his precious objects of entertainment on the side.

At the end they will show the drawings to each other and will be able to add more elements at the suggestion of their classmates.

This activity will stimulate imagination and creation, since AS children and adolescents will be able to perceive that things often go beyond what is superficially shown and that if they think about them carefully, they can create things and make them more fun.

15
THE BROKEN TELEPHONE

Materials needed for this dynamic: telephone

Minimum number of people: 20 and 25 people.

Time: approximately 40 minutes

The dynamic consists of creating a message through what they hear the other participants express.

The participants will be organized in a circle, standing side by side.

The leader of the group will stand in front of the first member, take the phone and in a low voice will give him/her a message, pass the phone to him/her, and the participant who received the message will repeat the action.

He/she must stand in front of the other member and with telephone in hand, repeat the message that the leader said, if he/she does not remember, then must create one as close as possible to the one he/she heard.

In this way, the telephone will be passed to each participant with a message, until the last one is reached.

When the last participant makes his or her intervention, generally the message would not be the same as the one transmitted by the leader.

They will then have the task of creating a new message, which at least resembles the first one, trying to build it with key words that each one has heard.

The aim is to stimulate the development of thinking and thus give rise to thinking differently, outside the patterns of everyday life.

16
THE BOAT SINKS

Materials needed for this dynamic: rope

Minimum number of people: 20 and 25 people.

Time: approximately 45 minutes

The objective of the exercise is to come up with ideas to help the sinking ship reach land safely.

Participants should make a big circle, then take the rope and make a circle around them, once everyone is inside the circle, close it with a knot.

The leader must make it clear that once the dynamic has started, each member must participate.

Everyone should begin to circle around the rope or rope, they can even move around inside the circle while the leader walking among them, says out loud: "the ship is sinking, the ship is sinking, what shall we do?"

At that moment everyone stops and one raises their voice to contribute an idea, example: "let's look for the life jackets," they all start to simulate looking for the life jackets and put them on.

The activity continues under the same dynamics, the leader continues walking among them saying: "the boat is sinking, the boat is sinking, what shall we do?"

They stop again and another participant takes the floor: "let's give each other a hug." So on and so forth until everyone has participated by contributing their idea to save the boat or survive the situation, including the Asperger's child or adolescent.

At the end, a small conclusion is made about the importance of creating and contributing our ideas, even in the most difficult moments.

17

I CREATE BY PAINTING AND BUILDING

Materials needed for this dynamic: plasticine or clay, leaves, pencils, colors.

Minimum number of people: 20 and 25 people.

Time: approximately 45 minutes

This dynamic will consist of drawing and building the object of interest for each participant with leaves, colors, plasticine or clay.

The group leader or captain will give instructions to the group and proceed to place them in pairs. He/she will indicate that they have the task of choosing an object that they consider important and that is of great value to them.

First, they should draw a model on the sheet of paper and color it, to make it more attractive and to have a clear idea of what they are going to build, then they should begin to shape it with the plasticine and clay.

When they finish their work, they should share it with the group and explain the value that the object has for them and the difficulty they may have had in designing it.

The idea of working in pairs is that if, for example, in the case of an Asperger's child or adolescent it is difficult to give structure and shape to their drawing and construction, they can find support in the suggestions provided by the partner with whom they are working.

This can help them to broaden their vision and thus give room for imagination and creativity.

Group dynamics to work on handling implicit social rules

If there is something that is very difficult for children and adolescents with Asperger's is managing un written social rules, which allows integration and adaptation to their environments.

This is one of the reasons why they become very lonely; people who are diagnosed with this syndrome lack appropriate social skills.

Their ability to understand a reciprocal conversation is very limited, so they do not seem to understand written rules and especially unwritten one susually learned through observation.

Diaz Elias, philosopher, indicated in 1997, that the inability of Asperger children to understand written rules, compromises their self-awareness, impulsivity control, cooperative work and concern for others.

For this reason, there is a need to offer strategies that allow them to adapt and thus improve their relationship with their environment.

20 POINTS TABLE

Materials needed for this dynamic: sheet of bond paper, colored markers.

Minimum number of people: 20 and 25 people.

Time: 45 to 60 minutes approximately

The dynamic consists of assigning a series of tasks to the group members, which will be related to the values that must be fulfilled every day in order to have a successful relationship with their environment.

Group participants will be instructed to take a sheet of paper, place their name in one of the corners and place it in a visible place in the space where they are performing the exercise.

This will consist of assigning some tasks that the participants must complete, and they can be given 4 or 5 minutes for each one.

One of the tasks can be that two people will make a drawing on a single sheet of paper, with a single group of colors, both should participate in the development of the assignment, here you can see that the values of sharing, solidarity, respect, others come into play.

For example, if someone wants to do the drawing alone without listening to his partner, or does not want to lend his colors, he will be asked to go to his sheet of bond paper and write what he does not want to do with a face that represents his emotion, sadness or anger.

If the unfulfilled rule is that they did not want to listen to their partner, their chart should indicate "I find it difficult to work as a team and draw a sad face next to it."

If, on the other hand, they manage to accomplish the task without major inconvenience then likewise, but in this case both of them, they should turn to their bond paper and place the tasks accomplished with their respective smiley face.

Then another assignment is given, to write together a short story about some real or imaginary fact, following the same dynamics, the work must be done together and so on. They can perform three or four assignments, which involve meeting standards by doing the work.

The idea is to reinforce the need to always comply with the rules in order to carry out a successful teamwork.

This dynamic can also address the issue of emotions, since any action, positive or negative that human beings perform will result in the appearance of a mood, which, like abiding by rules must be channeled in the best way in order to create empathy with the environment.

21
FOLLOW THE TRACK

Materials needed for this dynamic: sheets of paper, markers, plastic tape.

Minimum number of people: 20 and 25 people

Time: approximately 45 minutes

When participating in the activity, the AS child or adolescent will need to comply with the established rules in order to achieve the objective.

The leader or captain of the group will explain the rules of the dynamic to the participants. First, he/she will choose one of person in the group and explain that he/she was the one selected to look for the object that will be hidden in the space following a series of clues.

The chosen one must leave the place while the object is hidden and the clues that he/she must follow to start the search are placed on the floor.

Once the participant is outside, he/she will proceed to look for a place and hide the object to be found, also placing on the floor each and every one of the clues that must be followed to reach the goal.

The selected person is invited to enter the space again and follow the indications on the floor one by one, which will lead him/her to find what has been hidden.

Once he/she has succeeded, a space for reflection will be taken where emphasis will be placed on the activity carried out and how the participant, following the directions, can achieve the task.

The ultimate goal is that the Asperger child or adolescent, through observation, can understand the value of being able to abide by the rules that are established in our environment and these contribute to better communication and to achieve the goals set.

Dynamics to work on difficulty in understanding nonverbal communication

Children and adolescents with AS have difficulty understanding nonverbal communication, that which is expressed through gestures, facial expressions, tone of voice, and others.

This represents one of the great problems for their communicative process and, as a consequence, problems related to behavior, anger, frustration, not only in the one who suffers the syndrome, but also in those they interact with and their environment.

Fiuza Maria, psychologist, indicated in 2018, that nonverbal communication complements, emphasizes and regulates what is expressed verbally, a person with Asperger syndrome presents difficulty in understanding this, and therefore limits the transmission to a greater extent of the true feelings or moods of the other.

This situation has a direct impact on the ability to understand and express emotions.

22
FIVE AT A TIME

Materials needed for this dynamic: chairs and handkerchief.

Minimum number of people: 20 and 25 people

Time: approximately 30 minutes

The purpose of this dynamic is to allow the group to participate without the need to pronounce words, including children and adolescents with Asperger. The captain or group leader should distribute all participants in small groups of five people.

Five chairs will be placed in the center of the space, the first group should stand in front of them, at the beginning of the dynamic, they will count ten seconds and sit down on the chairs all at the same time, then count ten more and stand up. No one should utter a word.

If a partner makes a mistake or misses the count, the group has to indicate the time through gestures or signs.

The leader will be in front of them with a handkerchief. Throwing the handkerchief to the floor indicates that the group's turn is over and is now time for the other group of five.

In the same way, without words, they must indicate with gestures or signs that is time to move to the chairs.

The dynamics carries on. Ten seconds standing, ten seconds sitting, and they get up again following the thread of nonverbal communication. In this way, all the groups are given room to participate, until everyone has completed the task.

At the end, the leader will make a summary of the learning transmitted, explaining that even without using words, common verbal language, all human beings have the ability to express and communicate.

23
FIND YOUR PARTNER

Materials needed for this dynamic: paper, markers and plastic tape or pins.

Minimum number of people: 20 and 25 people.

Time: approximately 60 minutes

The leader provides each participant with a sheet of paper, a marker and a pin or piece of plastic tape. He/she will place on the board a group of different categories: music, fashion, movies, games, food.

Then he/she indicates that they must select a category and place its characteristics on the sheet with the markers. Each participant works without copying what the partner does -this first part is individual.

For example: the one who selects the music category, will place on his sheet, dance, moving, ballad, cheerful, couple, among others, note that not only characteristics should be placed. Each person will do the same.

Once finished, everyone must place their sheet on their chest in a visible way and will begin walking through the space reading to each other what everyone has onn their sheet.

People with similar characteristics will group together. They will take another sheet of paper and write in large letters the name of the category they represent, drawing a happy face for achieving the objective, and so on until they are all organized.

Then the leader will emphasize how nonverbal expression allows for communication.

24
THROUGH MIMICRY

Materials needed for this dynamic: notebooks, pencils, brooms and objects available in the space.

Minimum number of people: 20 and 25 people.

Time: approximately 30 minutes

The group participating in the exercise should sit on the floor in a circle.

The group captain will select several members and will give them a piece of paper with short messages that they must express to their companions without using words.

The Asperger's child or adolescent has the ability to learn many things through observation, so this dynamic is ideal to help them understand what is often transmitted through gestures.

The first participant is given the turn to stand in the circle and begin transmitting his or her message. For example, "I was writing in my notebook and my pencil broke, it made me very angry." He will look for a way to make himself understood to the group through mimicry until he himself, giving clues, gets the message right.

Then the other participant will pass: "I was sweeping and they stepped on my garbage, it made me very sad." One by one, the members who were selected will participate until the end of the dynamic, four or five people can be chosen for this purpose.

Once it is finished, the leader will talk to the group to find out how they felt, if deciphering the message generated some stress, if they had any difficulty or if it was an easy task. Thus, reinforcing the objective pursued through gestures there is always something you may be able to convey.

25
WINDMILLS

Materials needed for this dynamic: colored ribbons.

Minimum number of people: 20 and 25 people

Time: 30 minutes approximately

The dynamic will be developed with the participation of the whole group, the leader will give the indications so that it is carried out in harmony.

Then a space will be delimited where they are. They will have to start spinning around the space with their colored ribbons in hand pretending to be a windmill. If they collide with each other, they should express their feelings without words, but using gestures.

At the end, they will be placed in pairs and will comment on how they felt during the development of the dynamic and what were the emotions they experienced. Once the activity is over, they will form a large circle where everyone can participate by expressing their experience.

This will allow the Asperger's child or adolescent to understand that what each one expressed with their gesture was a way of communicating the feeling generated by being tumbled by others.

Group dynamics to address excessive interest in a given topic

Children and adolescents with Asperger's sometimes tend to show excessive interest in certain topics, which can interfere negatively in their interpersonal relationships, as well as in their learning, due to the time they spend researching about it.

Gomez Angel, psychologist, said in 2010, that children with Asperger syndrome, are obsessively focused in knowing content. They are limited in their thinking, which results in isolation from their social environment.

If you guide them appropriately, it is possible to make them understand that there are equally important scenarios to explore and that there is time for all of them.

26
THE MEETING

Materials needed for this dynamic: notebooks, pencils, folders, pens.

Minimum number of people: 20 and 25 people.

Time: 30 minutes approximately

The dynamic begins by explaining to the group that it will be a representation of a company meeting, where important people will meet to discuss issues related to it.

A group of participants, between 8 and 10, will be in charge of carrying out the representation while the rest plays the role of observers.

This can be repeated, choosing another group of participants, so that everyone participates in the activity.

A table or desk is placed in the center of the space with their respective chairs and the group that will be as observers will sit in a circle around them.

The selected group will be seated in the circle and the motivation for their meeting will be to talk about the development of the company, discussing specific topics related to the institution they represent.

They will discuss topics such as finances, production, economy, furniture, resources, employees, etc. Each participant will have a few minutes to give their point of view, the rest of the group observes and listens attentively around them.

After the time has elapsed, they conclude the session by emphasizing the importance of the plenary session and the need to address all the issues raised, they finish and give room to the other group to repeat the activity so that everyone can participate.

At the end of the dynamic, the leader will invite everyone to sit in a circle and ask questions about what they observed, guiding the interventions to the objective, which will be that all the topics and aspects that surround us are of great importance and that each one deserves a particular time of dedication.

If we focus our attention completely on one thing, we tend to neglect others, bringing negative consequences, and we will certainly have to spend time later on attending to them, thus delaying the processes.

27
THERE IS TIME FOR EVERYTHING

Materials needed for this dynamic: sheets of paper, notebook, pencils, colors.

Minimum number of people: 20 and 25 people.

Time: approximately 45 minutes

The group captain will indicate categories to the participants that they should characterize: food, music, games, entertainment, education, others, for the development of the group. For the development of each one, a specific time will be allotted.

Characteristics should not be very long, three or four that will allow to perceive what is being described. Colors can be used to identify and differentiate one from another.

After the time has elapsed, the leader should select at least five members, who will come to the front to explain what they have developed and the importance of the time dedicated to each one.

Then the child or adolescent with Asperger's will be chosen to explain what he/she did with the assigned task. The idea is that he/she first observes and listens to his/her peers in order to situate him/herself, and then speaks from his/her own experience.

The leader who carries out the dynamic will have the task of reinforcing and complementing what he expresses in order to make him understand that there are many topics of interest about specific things and that there is the possibility of approaching several at the same time to get to know them, without having to invest so much or all the time in just one.

28
WHAT DO I KNOW?

Materials needed for this dynamic: sheet of paper and pencil.

Minimum number of people: 20 and 25 people.

Time: approximately 45 minutes

The group leader will give each participant a sheet of paper and a pencil and will indicate that each participant should select a topic that interests him/her and write about it on the sheet of paper.

Once the time has elapsed, each participant should read what he/she wrote on the sheet, for example: "What do I know? I know about sports," and explain all the information he/she has about the topic.

This will be done successively until everyone has participated including the child or adolescent with AS.

When everyone has presented what they have written, the leader should reflect on the importance of knowing about other topics that are not only of interest to us.

There is a range of possibilities when it comes to learning and absolutely everyone is free to do so.

The topics of interest are fascinating, but with them there are other things that are also fascinating and worth knowing, this is the objective that is pursued, so that children and adolescents with the syndrome can open themselves to know beyond a simple approach.

29
TRIPLE ANSWER

Materials needed for this dynamic: sheets of paper and pencils.

Minimum number of people: 20 and 25 people.

Time: 45 to 60 minutes approximately

The captain leading the exercise will give each member a sheet of paper and a pencil, with which they must answer the question "What interests me?

The answers will involve writing down three different things that each person likes with their main characteristics.

After about 20 minutes, the stage is opened to allow participation with what each person has written.

The leader will ask them to come to the front five at a time and the rest will listen carefully.

One by one they will begin to narrate what interests them and what characterizes them. If within the group there is someone who is interested in what is being presented and knows more characteristics than those mentioned, he/she can raise his/her hand and participate to complement the information.

This dynamic intends that the Asperger child or adolescent learn about the diversity of topics that exist and are of great interest not only for the person who is considering it, but also for others, and that even when they have information about different topics of interest, they are not limited to learning about other things.

Group dynamics for working on resistance to change

Asperger children and adolescents have a very rigid way of thinking, for this reason it is very difficult for them to adapt to changes, as well as to understand the different points of view and alternatives expressed by others. They waste a lot of time following routines and ways of doing things that are not very useful.

Kanner Leo, a professional in psychiatry, in one of his many studies on autistic children considered in 1956 that they manifest an anxiously obsessive desire to keep things unchanged, which results in a marked limitation in a variety of spontaneous activities.

It is one of the particularities of children and adolescents with Asperger's that reduces their possibilities of integrating into their environment, which is why group dynamics are proposed as strategies that allow them to be open to change and enjoy the benefits of relating to others.

30
BALL WITH PHRASES

Materials needed for this exercise: ball

Minimum number of people: 20 and 25 people.

Time: approximately 40 minutes

The group leader or captain will tell the group to form a large circle in the space designated for the exercise.

Then he/she will take the ball and explain that each person should pass it to his/her partner expressing a simple and descriptive phrase, for example: "nice day," "rainy day," "blue sky," all the phrases expressed must have a meaning.

Once the dynamic has begun, the leader will let a short time pass while they pass the ball and become familiar with the different phrases they express, and when the time is up, he/she will stop and ask for the ball back to change the rule of the game.

Then repeat the activity, but this time the phrases they express must be related to the previous one, for example: "on this gray day," "and with so much cold," "I preferred not to go out," and so on until everyone has participated.

Once the exercise is over, a space is opened for reflection: What did they notice? How did the exercise begin? How did it end? Did it change? Which one? How did they feel? Which round was the most difficult and why? To conclude, emphasize the importance and the need to adapt to the changes that occur every day.

31

CHANGING THINGS AROUND

Materials needed for this dynamic: notebooks, pencils, markers, erasers, handkerchiefs, others available.

Minimum number of people: 20 and 25 people.

Time: approximately 45 minutes

The team leader will start the exercise, the members of the group should make a circle in the space designated for the exercise.

The leader will indicate that each one must visualize in detail where each object is located, the notebooks, pencils, eraser, markers, chairs, among others, while observing they must repeat aloud guided by him, the eraser is with the blackboard, the notebooks on the table, the pencils in Maria's hands, and so on.

When they finish, they will be instructed to place the handkerchief over their eyes, meanwhile the captain changes the objects from the place where they were.

Then he asks participants to remove the handkerchief from their eyes and asks: where is the eraser? The immediate reaction will bet or indicate the place where it was first before they can notice the changes.

When they become aware that the objects have been moved, they should do an observation exercise to adapt to the changes made, then they will start again to indicate out loud where each object is located.

The dynamic is repeated again so that they can adapt to the fact that every time they cover their eyes the objects will be changed of place, without doubts, in this second opportunity, when they are asked where is the eraser? The answer will not be immediate, they will first take the time to observe.

Changes are part of life and the human being walks with the ability to adapt to them, sometimes you just have to take some time to assume, without major inconvenience the new realities.

Asperger children and adolescents, with the guidance of their leader, will be able to understand the learning.

32
THE CLOCK

Materials needed for this dynamic: markers

Minimum number of people: 20 and 25 people.

Time: approximately 20 minutes

The dynamic will consist of making several changes that will allow the child or adolescent with Asperger's to open his or her thoughts to the changes that can happen in everyday life, even if they seem simple or insignificant.

The leader or captain will divide the group into two equal parts; then each group should make two circles holding hands with each other, then draw with their markers a huge clock on the board indicating that the time starts.

The first circle must take place in the space in an organized manner, then the second circle will be placed inside them, one in front of the other.

The dynamics will consist in that, at the leader's voice, both groups will start to turn around each other, but in different directions.

One group will turn to the left and the other to the right, at the leader's voice of change, they will have to change direction and start walking again.

This situation will be repeated for a few minutes, so that the participants understand the dynamics, adapt to the change and become familiar with the activity.

It may be difficult the first time around, but once they understand how the activity works, they will be able to do it with greater confidence.

After some time, everyone will take their place and there will be space for reflection, how did they feel? What lessons can they learn?

Everyone will have the right to participate and tell their experience, the Asperger child or adolescent will not only be seen as part of the dynamic because of their experience, but also by listening and observing the experience of others.

He/she will be able to understand that everyone, at some point, will be subject to some kind of change and that the important thing is to be able to adapt to them in the best way possible.

33

THE APARTMENT

Materials needed for this exercise: sheets of paper and colored markers.

Minimum number of people: 20 and 25 people.

Time: 45 minutes approximately

The dynamic begins by dividing the children or adolescents into groups of four people, they will be given sheets of paper and markers where they will write the words: walls and tenant.

At the end of this first time each one must assume a role, those who will be walls will be identified with the sheet that says walls and the one who will be a tenant will be identified with the one that says tenant.

The leader will explain the development of the dynamic, those identified as walls will make a little house with their hands and the one identified as a tenant will be underneath them.

When the leader says out loud: "tenants" all the tenants must leave their house and change houses, that is, look for another group that says walls.

When the leader says out loud: "walls" it will be the walls who run around the space looking for other tenants.

This action will be repeated several times, until everyone adapts to the changes and performs them with greater confidence. Once everyone has identified walls and tenants, the dynamics will be much simpler.

At the end, there will be time for reflection and participation so that everyone can tell and enrich each other with their experience.

Group dynamics to work on anger

Anger is one of the emotions that children and adolescents with AS often experience when they do not know how to cope with a situation.

Although a specific section has been dedicated to dynamics to work on emotions, it is necessary to make an individual space for anger management.

Children and adolescents with Asperger require tools that allow them to recognize and work on anger in themselves and in others, since the feeling of frustration is the first manifestation in an impulsive way, which uncontrolled can trigger aggression in themselves and others.

Cristiana Oroz, pedagogue and therapist, published in 2020, that children with Asperger's, daily present difficulties with things that for other children is normal. This brings as a consequence an overwhelming anxiety and frustration, with unavoidable feelings that surpass them and their only form of expression is through anger and aggression.

If they learn to channel them, then their experiences will be less frustrating and they will be able to assume their limitations in a more adequate way.

34
FREE YOURSELF FROM ANGER

Materials needed for this dynamic: balloons, leaves, pencils.

Minimum number of people: 20 and 25 people.

Time: 45 minutes approximately

The dynamics will begin with a space for reflection between the leader and the participants explaining what anger consists of, the acts that generate it and how it can be channeled.

This will be done in order to contextualize the dynamics so that everyone, including the Asperger child or adolescent, learns to identify it.

Once this space is closed, each member will be given a pencil and a sheet of paper on which they can write all things that make them angry.

When everyone has finished, each member will be given a balloon in which they will insert the paper and then inflate it.

With balloon in hand, they will leave the space where they are to a free space, the leader will explain that on the count of three everyone must release the balloons and let them go, in this way they will be saying goodbye to those things that generate anger in a symbolic way.

Then everyone will return to the space in order to close the activity generating a space for participation in which everyone can comment on their experience.

This conclusion should be oriented to the need to learn and understand that this emotion, correctly oriented, is normal in human beings and that channeling it as it should be, will help to improve interpersonal relationships.

35
THE ANGER BOX

Materials needed for this dynamic: sheets of paper, colored markers and a box.

Minimum number of people: 20 and 25 people.

Time: 45 to 60 minutes approximately

The dynamic will begin with the reading of a story about rage or anger by the leader.

One of the suggested readings is "what a tantrum" by Mireille de Allancé, which tells the story of a little girl who did incredibly bad at school, when she got home, nothing went as she wanted, when she finally burst into an uncontrolled anger, a giant monster came out of her destroying everything around her.

Realizing the disaster the monster had made the girl began to fix everything with a lot of patience and while doing so the monster shrunk until it disappeared.

At the end of the reading, a space for reflection will be opened in order to find out what they understood from the reading and what they think they learned from it.

After the intervention of a few people, not necessarily all of them have to intervene, they will be given a sheet of paper and markers, they will have to think about those situations that make them explode in anger, and represent it through a drawing.

When everyone has finished, they will be asked to add eyes, nose, mouth, hands and feet, so that they can visualize their own monster much more clearly.

A box will be placed in front of them, and the leader will ask each of them to get up from their seats and place their monster inside it. He will then indicate that is the box of rage and that monsters will be locked there and will not be able to bother again and that in case the monster appears again, they know he has a place to go.

The space for reflection is opened again so that everyone can verbally express their experience.

It should be explained to them that the monster of anger appears sometimes, especially when an objective is not achieved, but that it should not, in any way, overpower you. On the contrary, the person must subdue the monster and send it to the box. Also, that anger is a normal and common feeling that, if treated correctly and in time, can be easily controlled.

In addition, they can be explained that in a situation that generates anger, to immediately think of the box and in a symbolic way, send their monster there before it makes a disaster.

Asperger children and adolescents are very intelligent. Being able to observe and follow the dynamics step by step will allow them to find an ideal tool to channel their anger.

36

THE VOLCANO

Materials needed for this dynamic: sheets of paper and colored markers.

Minimum number of people: 20 and 25 people

Time: 45 minutes approximately

The dynamics is initiated by the leader explaining to the group the volcano eruption process. As he/she explains, the group is instructed to close their eyes to imagine it.

Then, similarities are established between the process of the volcano and that of anger, when a person begins to feel anger for something, in his stomach he will begin to feel heat and sensations around his stomach, which indicates that the volcano is about to erupt.

If they do not find a way to put out that fire, the lava will begin to boil, erupt and explode, burning everything in its path and making a disaster.

A huge volcano is drawn and colored on the blackboard, and participants are given sheets of paper and markers so that they can draw their own.

Once they have drawn it, they should include all the things that make them angry, they can exchange information in order to understand that anger is a feeling that everyone experiences and they can become familiar with the activity that the volcano performs.

Then they are instructed to stand up, a large circle is made and apart from it about 5 participants are selected to represent the lava that will make the volcano explode.

Participants in the circle must remain motionless and as the leader's shout: "The volcano is going to explode" those inside the circle will begin to spin around trying to get out, until they manage to move a few participants of the circle and get out of it by exerting pressure.

Amidst laughter, the space for reflection will be opened, this time inviting all the members to place themselves inside the circle where everyone can participate and express their experience.

The reflection should focus on explaining that the volcano never explodes all at once, which would have already been explained at the beginning of the dynamic and this time it will be mentioned as a way thore inforceit.

The volcano first initiates a process that cautions that it is about to erupt. The same way happens with human beings, nobody explodes without first giving some signals, for this reason it is necessary to be very attentive. This will allow to channel the anger avoiding that the volcano makes eruption.

37
I CALM DOWN

Materials needed for this dynamic: sheets of paper and pencils.

Minimum number of people: 20 and 25 people.

Time: 45 minutes approximately

The leader starts the dynamic by giving each participant a sheet of paper and a pencil and indicating that they should write on it those things that bother them intensely and that make them burst in anger.

The purpose of this first part is for them to identify how they really experience anger and how they react to it.

Then, they should form a circle, close their eyes and think about all the things they wrote on the sheet, and as they think, they will do a breathing exercise.

The calm and correct breathing takes people to a state of undisturbed tranquility.

As they remember and breathe deeply, the leader will ask: what do I think? what do I feel? what do I do?

As the leader speaks, the participants should respond to themselves, then substitute pleasant things or events for the thoughts.

The leader asks again: what do I think, what do I feel, what do I do?

After some time has elapsed during the exercise, the leader will ask everyone to return to their places to begin a space for reflection.

This will be oriented as follows: in the first part of the breathing, thoughts were focused on unpleasant events and three questions were asked: how did they feel and what was their response to them?

Space is opened for each one to share their experience, then reference is made to the second moment, they thought of pleasant things and how they responded, again giving room for the intervention of each participant.

At the end of the session, reference is made to the fact that in the face of unexpected events that occur on a daily basis, the most intelligent idea that can go through the mind is: "I calm down," there are situations that get out of hand, and outbursts of anger will not contribute to solve anything at all.

On the contrary, it can only generate serious inconveniences not only for the person experiencing the anger, but also for the environment.

Children and adolescents with Asperger's may understand that they will not always be in control of everything and that when faced with what they cannot solve, the best thing to do is to breathe and try to calm down, this will contribute to a better adaptation in the spaces in which they find themselves.

Group dynamics to work on hyperactivity or hypoactivity to certain sensory stimuli

Children and adolescents with Asperger's generally present an excessive sensitivity to certain sounds, smells, lights, etc., which contributes to a lack of attention in the activities they are willing to carry out.

Gabriela Matienzo, child psychologist, detailed in 2020, that children and adolescents with AS exposed to a lot of sensory stimulation may feel stunned, for this reason, they tend to react to them in a hyper or hypoactive way.

In general, they do not expose themselves because they know the discomfort that these exaggerated stimuli generate, however, they cannot always control what happens around them.

Through some dynamics it is possible to provide them with tools that allow them to act in the best way in the face of these events, in order to be in harmony with the demands of the environment.

It is worth emphasizing that the use of the dynamics will not diminish the discomfort generated by certain sensory stimuli, these will only help in the reaction they have to them, so that they can return to a state of calm.

38

GAME OF COLORS

Materials needed for this dynamic: sheets of paper, colored markers, scissors, small bell.

Minimum number of people: 20 to 25 people.

Time: 45 to 60 minutes approximately

The group leader will start the exercise by dividing the group into small teams of four or five people.

He/she will give each one sheets of paper, markers and scissors, on which the members of each team must draw small squares or figures and color them in different colors, these colors must be repeated, for example: 4 green, 4 yellow, 4 red, 4 blue and so on, according to the colors they have chosen.

Once all the cards have been created, the leader will start the activity, which will be developed team by team so that everyone participates.

The activity consists of developing the ability to concentrate on an activity.

They place themselves around the table and place a bell in the center of the table.

Each team that takes its turn, must place the colored squares on the table, one by one, leaving a color, everyone must observe carefully, when one of the colors has been placed 4 times, the first one to notice it must ring the bell.

All the groups and their members will have a turn to develop the task, when everyone has participated, the dynamics will stop and space will be opened for the corresponding reflection.

When the situations that occur around us disturb in a significant way there are always options to respond, and one of them is to take the attention away and focus it on something that generates peace.

Bringing the reflection directly to children and adolescents with Asperger's disease emphasizes those sensory situations that affect them so much, before them, with a little calm, they can direct their attention to something that is around them and produces them more interest.

If they manage to direct all their attention to another situation, the excessive sensory effect that disturbs them will surely pass into the background.

They are usually adept at turning their full attention to things or situations that they consider truly relevant.

39
ASSEMBLE THE CASTLE

Materials needed for this dynamic: wooden or cardboard blocks or squares.

Minimum number of people: between 20 and 25 people.

Time: 45 minutes approximately

The leader will start the activity by dividing the entire group of participants into two teams.

They will take the blocks or cardboard squares and begin to build a castle in the center of the space.

The idea is for everyone to participate and place the squares one on top of the other. If someone makes a mistake and the square they are placing falls down, they must dissolve the whole castle and start all over again.

The dynamic is concluded when one of the teams manages to place all the blocks without making a mistake.

This task requires a lot of concentration; making a mistake due to distraction causes the dynamic to start again and will cause them to waste a lot of time.

At the end of the exercise, a space for reflection is opened, where everyone will have the opportunity to participate and share their experience.

It is possible that having to start the dynamic over and over again due to distractions or mistakes generates stress, for this reason it is necessary to be completely focused on what they are doing.

It should be emphasized to Asperger children and adolescents that when they find themselves in a situation that disturbs them, the best task to flee from it is to focus all their attention on something that really attracts them and gives them peace back.

40
THE TURTLE

Materials needed for this dynamic: sound equipment and CD.

Minimum number of people: 20 and 25 people.

Time: 45 minutes approximately

This dynamic is very simple and provides tools for children and adolescents with Asperger's to regulate their behavior and hyperactivity.

The leader will indicate to the group members that they should stand in a circle, the dynamics will consist of being very active at times, and at other times they should assume the role of a turtle and remain calm.

The leader will play music and everyone should behave happily, they can play, dance, talk, talk, talk.

When the leader says out loud "the turtle" everyone should slowly bend down and put their hands up like a shell, while the leader slowly lowers the music until the whole space is silent and in complete peace.

The activity will be repeated several times so that the participants can identify with the two actions, one that makes them active and the other that gives them tranquility.

At the end of the activity, everyone is given the opportunity to express how they felt while they were doing the dynamic and to what daily situation, they can relate it to.

Once everyone has intervened, they will be referred to the slight movements of the turtle, who when it feels a threat, moves slowly and acts little by little, while hiding in its shell and calming down.

You cannot always have control over everything that happens outside, but you can have control over how you react to these events.

41
WHAT IS MISSING?

Materials needed for this dynamic: pencils, markers, books, notebooks, sheets of paper, erasers, texts, others.

Minimum number of people: 20 and 25 people.

Time: approximately 45 minutes

This dynamic is related to memory and allows children and adolescents with Asperger's to develop their ability to concentrate, using it as an escape strategy in the face of certain sensory stimuli that disturb them.

The leader will indicate to all participants that they should stand in a circle side by side.

In the center of the space, a table will be placed with different objects on it, pencils, notebooks, books, markers, sheets, erasers and all the objects that the participants themselves can provide.

Once all the objects have been placed, a participant is chosen and shown the number of objects on the table, he/she is instructed to mention them out loud and to do his/her best to memorize them in the place where they are located.

Then the child is asked to close his eyes, and at that moment the leader removes an object from the table, the child is asked to open his eyes again and observe, the child must say which object has been removed.

The game can be made more complex by adding more objects, reducing the time to memorize or removing more than one object.

Another member can also be given the opportunity to participate.

At the end of the activity, they will be asked about their experience with the dynamics, making reference to how important it is to keep the attention on the things that are relevant and leave aside what seems more disturbing and interferes with the tranquility.

Memory exercises are excellent strategies for children and adolescents with Asperger's, helping them to keep their attention on the things that are really important.

Being able to have strategies as a means of escape from those situations that generate so much disturbance, such as exaggerated sensory stimuli, will allow them to immediately locate themselves and maintain tranquility.

It is worth remembering that these strategies will not modify the way they act before certain stimuli, inevitably, within their characteristics and particularities of their condition, it is in them to act this way.

The dynamics will help them to remain calm in these situations, here they are presented as a group, but with proper guidance from their representatives, they can be adapted according to the needs of each one of them at the time they are required.

Group dynamics to work on motor skills

Children and adolescents with AS tend to suffer from motor difficulties that sometimes make them act clumsily in their movements.

This type of motor problem is related to fine motor skills, which is reflected in a variety of situations: through writing, lack of dexterity to catch a ball, a strange rhythm when running, difficulty getting dressed, tying their shoes, as well as buttoning buttons.

Estela Crissier, teacher and researcher, published in 2017, that children with AS present deficiency in their motor skills, which manifests when performing activities that involve these skills.

However, although this is a very particular characteristics of children with Asperger's, it is possible to work with specific strategies that help them to improve it and in turn be incorporated into the activities of their environment.

42
FOLLOW THE FOOTPRINT

Materials needed for this dynamic: cardboard, book, tape, adhesive and markers.

Minimum number of people: 20 and 25 people.

Time: approximately 30 minutes

The leader will start the exercise by explaining how it will be carried out.

He/she will divide the group into two teams and will provide them with cardboard, tape and markers, they will have to draw, paint, cut out footprints, once this first part is done, they will stick them on the floor with the tape, from one end of the space to the other.

The dynamics will consist of the following: the team is subdivided into two small groups, one row is placed at the beginning, where the footprints begin and the other where they end.

The one who starts the dynamic places a book on his head, takes an object, it can be a pencil, a notebook or a marker and walking little by little following each one of the footprints that are stuck on the floor, he must give it to his partner who is waiting for him at the other end.

He receives and returns the same way, and gives the object to the partner waiting for him on the other side, with the book on his head.

So on and so forth until three or four objects have been exchanged. The team that finishes sharing first is the winner.

At the end of the dynamic, the group gathers to make the pertinent reflection, this should be oriented to the importance of the development of certain physical activities, since they contribute to improve motor skills, developing abilities that allow interactionwith others in larger spaces.

43
COLORED RINGS

Materials needed for this dynamic: colored rings, markers, bond paper.

Minimum number of people: 20 and 25 people.

Time: 45 to 60 minutes approximately

The dynamic is initiated by the team leader indicating to all the participants how it will be developed.

The group should be divided into two large teams and these, in turn, will take 10 minutes to choose and talk about a topic that is of interest to everyone, such as food, recipes, music, fashion, games, etc. The two teams should interact with each other.

The two teams should interact with each other to choose the same topic, the idea is that everyone can participate.

Once they are ready, they will take the colored rings and place them on the floor, in two rows, from one end of the space to the other.

The theme selected by the teams will be written in marker on the blackboard, if available, or on a sheet of bond paper in a visible way, so that both teams can see it.

The leader, depending on the topic chosen by the participants, will ask a series of questions, the teams will be located in front of him at the other end.

One participant from each team must go in the direction of the leader in order to answer the question, they must jump over the hoops that are placed on the floor.

The participant who arrives first will be the one in charge of answering the question, losing the opportunity to the one who arrives later.

In the case of the Asperger's child or adolescent's turn, he/she can go through the hoops in the company of a companion who generates confidence in him/her and who can feel the support, in the same way to give the answer to the question, to be the first to arrive.

This act will be repeated with different questions so that everyone can participate.

At the end of the dynamic, the leader should make a short reflection on the importance of looking for activities that contribute to the development of gross motor skills.

44
CREATE THE GARLAND

Materials needed for this activity: roll of thread and buttons.

Minimum number of people: 20 and 25 people.

Time: approximately 45 minutes

This type of exercise is ideal for fine motor work in children and adolescents with Asperger's. The leader instructs the participants to work on their fine motor skills.

The leader indicates to the members that they must form two teams, these in turn, will take the roll of son and each one must have a button in hand.

The leader indicates in a loud voice: "start the dynamic" each team should begin to form its garland passing the child through the holes of the buttons, one by one until reaching the end.

Once the first part is finished, they will proceed to remove the thread from the holes again, each button must remain in the hands of its owner.

A second round is given, the leader must again indicate in a loud voice: "start the dynamic," the two teams will again begin to pass the thread through the holes, one by one until the garland is completely woven.

The leader can indicate another round or the end of the round, the team that manages to weave the garland the most times will be the winner.

This dynamic for children and adolescents with Asperger's is very useful, depending on the size of the hole of the buttons, it can become easier or more complex. The truth is that, as a strategy for the development and improvement of fine motor skills, it can be put into practice many times.

The end of the activity, as always, should conclude with a reflection, all the dynamics developed are applied with an objective and at the end, it should be verified that the learning was acquired by the participants.

45
WHAT TIME IS IT, MR. WOLF?

Materials needed for this dynamic: colored chalk.

Minimum number of people: 20 and 25 people.

Time: 45 minutes approximately

The leader will start the exercise by explaining how it will be developed.

The first thing to do is to take the colored chalk and delimit a space within the space where they are, this will be the wolf's cage, here he will place each of the participants that he manages to catch.

Then choose one of the participants who will play the role of the wolf.

The leader will start the dynamic, the children will be playing in the space and the wolf will be walking among them, the children will ask him what time is it, Mr. wolf, "Five o'clock" or any other time.

So they will do this at different times until the wolf deems to answer, "It's time for lunch."

When the wolf gives this answer, the children will start running all over the space, running away from the wolf. They have no place to hide, so they will have to run until the clock strikes twelve.

The clock will be represented by the leader who must count to twelve indicating the wolf's hunting time.

The children who are caught must remain in the cage until the end of the game, the rest will continue to participate until the child or children, who after several attempts, are not caught.

Once the dynamic is over, a space for reflection is opened, indicating how necessary are the activities that imply physical effort for the development of motor skills, even more so in children and adolescents with Asperger's who require strategies that allow them to develop them in the best way and thus be incorporated into the different activities.

Group dynamics to work on literal language comprehension

Children and adolescents with Asperger's usually interpret language in a literal way, so they can misinterpret expressions, phrases or facts, also they do not usually understand communication through metaphors, the same happens with jokes or words with double meanings.

Mas Maria, neuropediatrician, expressed in 2016, that in children with ASa rigid and often literal language can be appreciated, which has a negative impact on the development of their interpersonal relationships.

Since they do not understand that expressions sometimes are used as jokes, they may feel offended and even react violently, or otherwise limit, much more, the communication process.

Encouraging the development of group dynamics will allow them to observe that sometimes there is room to express themselves through jokes or metaphorical ways of conveying a message.

46
THE HAT

Materials needed for this dynamic: paper hats of different colors.

Minimum number of people: 20 and 25 people.

Time: approximately 45 minutes

The leader will start the exercise by explaining that people should be very attentive to the activities that will be carried out, because some messages will be transmitted that everyone should decipher.

He will take five hats, each of a different color, and place them on the desk, explaining the meaning of each one on the blackboard.

Yellow represents joy, white represents tranquility, red represents energy, blue represents intelligence and black represents sadness.

Then he will select five participants who will have to act out a scene from everyday life according to the color of each hat.

While each express himself/herself, everyone must listen attentively, he/she must tell a story using indirect expressions, metaphors, examples, and others.

The student who is able to identify what he/she is expressing, raises a hand and with the leader's permission, stands up and places the hat of the color he/she considers to be related to his/her message.

In this way, the five chosen members will have the opportunity to participate successively. At the end, a space for reflection is opened and the participants who placed the hats on their companions should explain what made them understand that the hat placed on them was the right one.

The leader will reinforce his intervention by confirming that expressions do not always have to be literal in order to be understood and that not everything that is expressed with indirect words should be misinterpreted. They are forms of communication and must be adapted to them.

The Asperger child and adolescent will be able to initiate a process of understanding through observation and participation in the dynamics.

47
PEPITO GOT SICK

Materials needed for this exercise: handkerchiefs, colored ribbons, glasses and other objects that the participants may wish to use.

Minimum number of people: between 20 and 25 people.

Time: 45 minutes approximately

The leader will indicate to all the participants that they must make a big circle. He will give them a message, which they must pass one by one and they in turn must explain it in different ways. They should include an emotion, romanticism, love, pain, joy, sadness, stress, others, any form and emotion they want.

Start the dynamic with the message in the leader's voice: "Pepito got sick," the member next to him should continue repeating the phrase, but with an emotion included, for example: "Pepito got sick" with laughter, followed by the one next to him, "Pepito got sick" with tears.

But with the particularity that the one who does it with joy should take the colored ribbons, the one with sadness a handkerchief, the one with stress a glass in the hand, all with an object that they can use to express their message, and so on until everyone has participated.

The activity should conclude with a teaching. There will bedroom for reflection and whoever likes can participate and express what he/she observed during the development of the activity. Also, it should be referred that many of the expressions that we observe as part of daily life are expressed in this way, and sometimes it is difficult to understand what the other person wants to transmit and even more so if it is not expressed literally.

However, this does not have to be a problem. Human beings have the capacity to understand others, and even if the expression isn't clear there is always an opportunity to ask. If it is something important, the other person most likely will clarify.

Asperger's children and adolescents are very intelligent and will surely understand the teaching.

48

THE MOTORCYCLE

Materials needed for this dynamic: helmets made of leaves.

Minimum number of people: between 20 and 25 people.

Time: 30 minutes approximately

This dynamic is very funny, as it shows that laughter produced by jokes in everyday life is healthy and that not every type of conversation between people always includes literal language.

The leader tells the group to form pairs, they ride on a motorcycle, put on paper helmets and one stands behind the other, the one in front extends his hands as if to take the handle and the one in the back takes him by the waist.

The one in front must imitate the sound of the motorcycle ruumm, piiiiiiii with a noise, while the one in the back guides him around the space.

The leader will count a prudential time while everyone moves at the same time, others collide, others brake, surely the laughter will be heard throughout the space.

The leader indicates that the time is over, that everyone must park their bike, get off and stand in a big circle.

It opens space for reflection and shows the need that human beings have for these spaces for recreation, laughter is healthy and represents well-being.

49
CONDUCTING THE ORCHESTRA

Materials needed for this dynamic: pencils

Minimum number of people: between 20 and 25 people.

Time: approximately 45 minutes

The dynamics of the orchestra allows its members, including children and adolescents with Asperger's, to open up to a space of relaxation and laughter therapy, making them understand that they are necessary in their daily lives.

The leader will indicate to the participants that it is time for the orchestra. The leader will lead the orchestra, and the members of the group will be the instruments, and at the signals given by the leader they should make their sounds.

If the right hand goes up, they should sound hahahaha, if the left hand goes up, they should sound hehehehehe, if both hands are extended forward, they should sound jojojojo, and if both hands go down, they should be silent.

The leader's movements can be fast, slow, crossed, the intention is to generate a space for fun.

The dynamic will conclude when the leader lowers his hands and ends the dynamic.

He/she will proceed to gather them in a circle in order to share their experience and enjoyment of the activity.

The children and adolescents with Asperger's will be able to observe that non-literal type of language is also part of the normality of the human being.

Group dynamics to work on excessive worrying

In general, children and adolescents with Asperger's syndrome have traits of excessive worry, they always want to have everything under control, knowing future events helps them to control their anxiety levels. According to the Coalition for Asperger Syndrome in the United States, one of the characteristics of this syndrome is that they get involved in obsessive routines and present peculiar worries.

There are situations that they may be able to handle given the discipline that characterizes them, but there are others that tend to get out of hand and they must understand that nothing happens, things are not going wrong and everything has a solution.

Providing them with tools and strategies helps them deal with uncertainty so that they enjoy life with greater peace of mind.

50
FLYING

Materials needed for this dynamic: pencils

Minimum number of people: 20 and 25 people.

Time: approximately 45 minutes

The leader will start by explaining the dynamic.

They will have to repeat several actions as per the leader's voice, for this, everyone will form a big circle. The leader will be inside it walking among the group, when he says "flying," all with their pencils in hand, they will raise them and start flying.

Then little by little he will mention a series of animals that fly, when he mentions them they will raise their hands and repeat the action, when he mentions another animal that does not have wings, they will lower their hands.

This will be repeated as many times as the leader deems necessary and according to the number of animals mentioned. The level of complexity may vary according to the speed with which the leader makes the changes when naming the animals.

At the end of the activity, there will be time for reflection, and participants will be asked how they felt during the activity. Surely for many, the fact of making changes may have generated some concern about making a mistake.

The leader should explain that these are the situations to which he/she is exposed on a daily basis, there are things that can be calculated and planned, but there are others that cannot.

Or maybe situations can be organized, but that does not mean that they will go as planned, it is possible that some eventuality may arise that changes or undoes the plans and that, as human beings, without anxiety or concern, we must find ways to make certain adaptations.

Children or adolescents with AS are fully capable of understanding the teaching that you want to convey through the dynamics in this case that in the face of what cannot be controlled, it is better to remain calm.

Made in United States
Orlando, FL
22 April 2024